MONOLOGUE OF A DEAF MAN

Also by David Wright

★

MORAL STORIES: POEMS

BEOWULF
(*Penguin Classics*)

THE FABER BOOK OF TWENTIETH
CENTURY VERSE

DAVID WRIGHT

MONOLOGUE OF
A DEAF MAN

ANDRE DEUTSCH

FIRST PUBLISHED 1958 BY
ANDRE DEUTSCH LIMITED
12-14 CARLISLE STREET SOHO SQUARE
LONDON WI
© DAVID WRIGHT 1958
ALL RIGHTS RESERVED
PRINTED IN GREAT BRITAIN BY
TONBRIDGE PRINTERS LIMITED
TONBRIDGE KENT

TO PHILLIPA REID

A Roman Emperor forbade
All public demonstration of
 A private love;
But, dedicating, I declare
Whatever poems written here
 Are for yourself
That you accept and overlook
 Both lie and book
And damn the absolute emperor.

ACKNOWLEDGEMENTS

Some of these poems appeared in the following anthologies and periodicals:
Botteghe Oscure (Rome), *Encounter, The Hudson Review* (U.S.A.), *New Poems 1955, New Poems 1956, New Poems 1957, Poetry Chicago* (U.S.A.), *Time and Tide, Peninsula* and *Nimbus;* and some have been broadcast in the B.B.C. Third Programme.

CONTENTS

A VOYAGE TO AFRICA

La vraie terre natale est celle où on a eu sa premiére émotion forte.

RÉMY DE GOURMONT

I

Adamastor, whom Camoens and the sea
Invented, was a giant who, we are told,
With Achilles' future mother wished to lie,
But met with a fool's mate colder than the snows
To become a seamark over Table Bay

Because the young lady turned him into stone.
You, my dear Adamastor, I invoke
(A myth, but the first immigrant European)
To come out from under your white tablecloth,
And, if you like, to bless the following poem.

Your outlook, bony and magnificent, leans
Upon waves fanning towards the deader pole,
The irreconcilable and married oceans,
With a real authority, superb and full,
With visions of a continent of penguins.

On your right, like gods or angels in a play,
Some Portuguese seamen, followed by some Dutch,
With sails and guns made their romantic entry
(But read Buffon upon female Hottentots)
And thus began South African history;

While on your left, or sinister, side there sleep
The bones of Dingaan's brother, and of Dingaan –
May their siesta prove unpleasant, and not light,
That nothing may discommode the present plan
Of many blacks labouring to make a white.

I, who left England upon St Lucy's day
And longest night, am undertaking to tell
In verses of a voyage to Africa;
And you, Adamastor, although somewhat dull
And deaf, must help to sustain me if I fly;

For I, born in fields you turn your back upon,
Lying between Sahara and Cape Aguilhas,
May legitimately claim to be your son.
You'd have preferred the fathering of Achilles –
Acquiesce in your destiny of a stone!

As quiet has been my fortune and your gift,
We should collaborate. Let me now begin.
At Northampton, in a high school for the deaf,
I was reading about Adonais, when
A whole Europe was engaged in peace,

Seesawing like a hesitant suicide
Before the act. O world of my adolescence
Not altogether entitled to regard,
But less completely black than the midwinter's
Night at Tilbury when I waited for the tide

And the hemispheres that now keep war on ice
Lay asleep, folded in a total gloom
As Thames, bearing down his comment to a rise
Of waters from a deep and shallow ocean,
Carried what fell so easily from my eyes.

That slumbering island with some stars disposed
Possessed me. While the river, seaborne, moved
Lost in a night's profoundest and longest shade,
On either side of the water slept or grieved
Those that made and loved me that I loved and made.

So, loving island, towering west and north,
She encompassed with sad massive arms my sleeping.
What is a man's birthplace? Where the man came forth.
Not where his embryo, dangerously leaping,
Arrives naked at an accidental hearth.

In no other way I acknowledged my home
Than by knowing her immense, and as a bride
Exhausted and fulfilled, when at her groin
I lay that night near and distant to her side
And left her in darkness to embark alone.

Beginning with a vision of division
Morning broke shrouded in gunmetal mist.
The sea, frog-throated, duffled its horizon;
Rehearsing, our engines trembled, paused, and stopped.
Vessels make an impression as a prison

And some may have been built to that image.
Mine, with cargo of importance and exile
Making a contemporary pilgrimage,
Hygiene, cash, defeat of boredom, being goal,
Voyaged through fog first, whooping like a savage

Across the Bay of Biscay to discover
The hills of Finisterre for Christmas morning.
A preparatory jostle from the weather
Set iron girders and the engines grinding
As wind bounced bareback upon rearing withers,

The ocean a welter. Europe lay to port
And guttered in sunrise, while the storm, half-blown,
Dragging its rage in flickering rags, trailed out
Its gales into the morning that Christ was born
And lost, in an irritable sea, my boat.

The apparition of Europe seemed final
When sea, with many lolling sky-coloured tongues
Circled the ship, my centre, with no landfall
To sever the reiterated horizons.
My vessel, chained to the zeroes like a ball,

Bobbed in a dandled basin of the doldrums
As approaching constellations, white and black,
Paid out their cable over the altered rims
Of heaven reflected in a sparking wake,
To modulate, night by night, its gaudy rooms

Till from the blue long barrows of the ocean
Emerged a purple and undelectable
Monolith, whose volcanic origin
Lends denial and a countenance to fable:
A mountain drawing thunderclouds and seamen.

Gabled and dun, where lie your woods, St Helena?
Where, island, do you support your oranges?
You that carry goats and men, but trees no longer,
Sing through the surges that those losing changes
Arrived with João da Nova Castella.

Midway to after and before, you, between
Africa, Europe, and the Americas,
Appear an omphalos, Janus-eyed island.
Can you recall a mutilated Portuguese,
Lopez? Does anything of the man remain

Among depilated hills? I felt your sea-gong
Everywhere in a multiple of valleys
Re-utter syllables, perhaps his name,
A misanthrope and a farmer of sorrows.
'Fernando, Fernando,' may be the sermon

That breezes fumbling over the clinker steer
To gnawn dingles, stagnant and as brown as oil;
'A one-fisted renegade without an ear,
Fernando Lopez, first inmate of exile,
Inhabited with an absolution here.'

We, the visitants, the immigrants, and those
Who, fed with the familiar, demand the same
In new environs, but at a lower price,
Thus wandering down a groove, always become
At a point of a voyage, or of our lives,

Aware we are looking back no longer to
Where we have come from, but must begin to plan
Arrival at those places to which we go –
As you, stark island, who marry European
To African dilapidation, seem to do.

For can flinging rope rings into tubs grow stale?
When the last land gull had abandoned our wake,
We, undisturbed by a bird or dolphin-school,
Exercised ourselves as usual upon deck
And daily dropped more grommets in the pail.

Now the sea had assembled over St Helena
And our mainmast, that spiked night and Orion
Who, exhaling, wore Betelgeux as a star,
Had bisected the great southern constellation,
Turbines and boredom groaned towards a shore

Which (a superb thunder over Table Bay,
Behind whose colours much ground, much of trouble,
Lies for who come, and for my fathers lay
Smiling upon the daylight of arrival)
Appeared indifferently out of Africa.

II

To come to a natal place and different faces
As a revenant, corrupted and aware,
Having weathered adolescence and voyages;
Thus to revisit a native city, where
Exiguous views equate the open spaces,

Questions have both answers, either black or white,
Where nothing adds up except, perhaps, the bill –
Shake, hero! Hero? Every man is that.
It resembles, since it is, descent to hell,
Therefore let the treatment of that theme be light.

Since no persons and no places understand
Anyone so well, or with so many lies,
As those environs in which his life began,
There to return is not to be pleased, nor please,
Where each unpleasable ghost turns into man,

You Perseus with the embarrassing head!
Who ever could be a prophet in his own – ?
Hero, when paying a visit to your dead,
There's no shadow to be seen then, except one,
Who dogs the alive disturber with its pad.

A cowardice and a courage brought me here,
Those elements that compel us to decide
Justly upon the choices that never were.
We make our destinies. Our destinies hide.
We create them who resist and yield to our

Natures, and who to allow or disallow
The evil and the good, depend on grace,
On what includes a farthing and a sparrow.
The holy gamble of the heavenly race
Betting against a certainty of sorrow.

When upon a Sunday morning I once more
Set foot upon what, to prohibit cross
Purposes, I term my natal not native shore,
European, literate, without a police
Record, and as officially free as air,

The sunlight beat like shades of a prison-house.
Those who restrict a liberty, restrict
The lot. Liberty is anonymous.
When invisible and general she exists,
As each undomesticated creature knows.

I was given reliable advice.
'In this country do as we do, as in Rome.'
I took that counsel but disliked my place
Set among discomfort earmarked European;
Yet discovered these arrangements were first-class

After a Europe spent in travelling third.
Abandoned by beasts and blackened by the light,
Veld careering under carriage wheels reverbed
The thousand hills and the length of day to night,
The drought and thunder to Johannesburg.

Pillars of salt about you, human city,
Glister against a blue and fortunate air.
We must love the impositions that you levy,
So deep to extend them, mother and vampire!
Bestower and subtractor of our vanity

Who thus, gridironed with concrete and wire,
Turns to the sky a naked disastrous face
Acknowledging the error of a power
That, one Eden, rigged a labyrinthine base
Deeper than gold, than her last galleries lower.

Here I was born. And here, like asparagus,
The small aspirations claw a higher sky
With commodities of an unchanged progress
Toward the exhaustion of the means to die.
Black, here, is the actual colour of distress:

Black as an adder to fear and to comfort.
The great American saloon cars blast by
Illustrious. As the summer ends the drought,
Summer its pandemonium gathers high
In purple cumuli over Magaliesberg.

An immaterial default will not perturb
Above undermining and minotaur caverns
The city which, without centre but a suburb,
Dishonoured by the distances and heavens,
Apparently proliferates and prospers.

By day the rocks, inhuman, flash from their hill
Or sweat with rain above this mortifying
City which I must inhabit; these appal;
O human city in a wilderness lying,
Holy about you night and lightning fall.

Here I was born, and here I am come back
To meet the consolation she provides.
That glittering white sierra, where neglect
Perpetuates an empire which she denies,
Swans on the silent border of a lake

Where thunder hangs, and so surrounds and threatens
With an accusation of rejected dust.
Let not rejection be a consolation.
Lose but not loose me, and I am not lost
To glory on the mines of desolation

That, thrown up by a Witwatersrand, outlie
The city where I was born, Johannesburg,
Balanced between the plateaux of a sky
And the deep ground; miserable as superb,
Common as divine, and like humanity.

Where by Orange Grove mimosas are cut down
And some orchards fallen to the building plots,
I abide by what proves to be not my home
Part of this journey. Let Moselekatse
Nek notched to the Magaliesberg mountain plume

Keep tally if I hear the goldfinches call
Above green cedar branches upon whose trees
I felt, first, a purgatorial silence fall,
Second, the consolation that always is
That all is well and shall console us all.

III

How gentle, courteous, and noble is nature
Whose beasts, when visible, appear dumb and good,
And whose prospects, munificent but pure;
Or she is cruel if that should be the mood,
May be dressed in or divested of allure.

A mirror more perfect than any of glass
She is: when looked in, the looker sees a shape
Of his emotion, and of what really was
There, looking in; of an angel or an ape.
If her mountains lean toward beguiling us –

In whom, once, we saw a visage of our fright,
Though long ago, and in another country,
Whereas today they flatter us with their height –
O nature, mirror or mishandled pantry,
Or medicine, goddess, enemy, what you like –

I love you, and knowing whom I really love,
I find it difficult not to love you more;
Either in a city's confines, at one remove,
Or when I, travelling past in train or car,
Touch the innocence your wildernesses prove.

As for the human spectators there on show
(Whose stink of worry, effectively overcome
By a scent of steel and petrol, does not now
Terrify to a stampede the herds of horn)
Become beasts by virtue of machines, they go

By Sabi in the Kruger National Park
Where the lions, mewing from Pretorius Kop,
And light-bummed impala, poised as a photograph,
Live easy as in an Eden, have no hope;
Content with joy infects with joy their dark.

Cropping under rocks depending for their fall,
Sunlit, the prelapsarian creatures move;
In their incommunicable selfish toil
They praise what made them with no need to love
Or ever to manifest that praise at all,

As we are led, by what I am now aware
Is guilt of loving not enough, to beg pardon,
Embarrassed by overmuch of love and care
And so excluded from the encircling garden,
In learning and in the laud of what moves there.

The hairy and stupid beasts that have no troubles
Beyond rinderpest and acts of God, increase.
A hippo, lulled by water, is snoring bubbles
While lion beside the zebra loll at peace;
Scavenging from heaven, an aasvogel wobbles;

And intelligent babooneries alone
Who peer from behind their thrones of boulders, pierce
The simple human disguise of a machine,
Avoiding the direction of eyes and ears
And of a curiosity like their own.

Here, virginal, without a memory, or
Regret, and balancing like a week's wash
Her clouds of summer over what cause affords,
The thorn-appointed veld unlids that face
The kraals of Umgungundhlovu rose towards,

And with not easily felt neutrality
Wields the indifference of a regard
That, deafer than a wilderness or the sky,
Seems yet to have seen where each black beast and guard
Makes shift, at night, in secret, towards its day.

About to fly of a midnight to England
I half turn, affected as a lover, while
Exiled I quit what seems a native ground,
Engage, already exiled, on an exile
With a half mad Europe to my northern hand;

Which to inherit, flying far and over
Johannesburg – above whose black defiles
The street lamps burn as I again remember
(O delectable in dark, luminous under hills)
That every farewell is in fact for ever –

A leaning plane's wing lifts me swiftly further.
In her long gown of evening she drags away,
And far lights flutter to a broad tiara.
Obscure, below, prodigious, and gothic, lie
The expanses galloping to a grand Sahara.

TO HIS PATRON

FROM HORACE

Why make me miserable with your whimper?
For neither the gods nor I myself desire,
    Prop and credit of what I am and do,
    That of the two you should be first to go.

Should an unlucky accident sequester
You, who are half my life, why should I loiter?
    I would be neither so beloved, nor whole.
    When death falls, then upon both let it fall.

This is my true parole, that we, whenever
You take the lead and go, depart together;
    Prepared, that supreme journey of the end,
    To travel as companions hand in hand.

And neither shall the fire speaking lion
Sever us, nor that many fingered giant
    Gyas, should he rise to stop my way.
    This, the three fates, and cogent justice, say.

Whether Scales, or horrid Scorpion, or He-Goat
Ruler of the western sea, my horoscope
    Rule as the influence of my birth hour,
    Our destinies are tethered star to star;

For, outglittering sad Saturn, Jupiter
Rescued you in the applauding theatre
    When the god hackled the quick wing of fate
    As, for the third time, the great rabble clapped.

And I have been barely missed, myself, by death;
Had not Faunus, when the tree pitched on my head,
    Faunus, who protects poets, Mercury's
    Companions, turned aside the falling tree.

ON A THIRTY-FIFTH SPRING

TO RALPH ABERCROMBIE

Among the excited and new leaves
I understand for the first time
How I am in the wrong season;
More than what is personal grieves
When, in this perturbation
Of cotyledon, egg, and beast,
I face October everywhere
While May assembles as it must.

It is not that the senses cringe
As the contracted days expand.
This frightens, but it is not all.
More than what is personal stings
When, opening on an April,
The apple valleys, blank as snow,
Declare an equinox, and are,
Till, guttering, their blossoms go

As gales more autumnal than those
That jar against November elms
Whirl, spin, and raze away the glory
Unrestorable by a rose.
At the watershed of a story
Mortal these intimations lie
About me as, grinning with fear
What has been born prepares to die.

Prepare a consolation then,
Words, words, by whose tough auguries
The generations live and go;
Sing, sing, in repetition
A memory we do not owe,
Which is the memory we share
United and half sundered from
That creation whose we are.

This mess of burgeon, let it raise
What must sink deeper to the mud;
And let the fury of this spring
Conjure, in its compelling praise,
What among dust would not, to sing:
He knows, against his will, that all
He may conjecture is a lie,
Although the great destruction fall.

Multiplication of each leaf,
Of every bird the air bereaving
To make a syllable of joy,
May rob the blocked heart of grief
Shut in its unforseeing eye,
As April whistles up a wind
That gathers all into her breast,
And every creature after kind.

STANZAS LOOKING BACK ON
ADOLESCENCE AND A LANDSCAPE

That he remembers those
Long travelled over lines
Thorn, poplar, oak, and rise
Bare under bare Malverns
As by his door today;

That he remembers them
Here who is long away,
Far gone in miles and time –
Rain drying on a leaf,
Dirt sticking to a limb,

Landscape, adolescence,
All the unharnessed then
Fury that blew about –
Means he may recognize
Not merely a divine

Wilder energy, but
Indeed a settled will
To thrust an importance
On each important hill
Seen to importunate.

The god of being laid
His living finger on
Turnip and discontent.
Who saw the spire fall
Bent by a sailing cloud?

Pimples and ignorance.
In that unhappiness
He was happier then –
No need a cloud or leaf
So shaken to acclaim

Because he shared the grief.
He has a language now:
Looks with what boredom on
A sparrow on a twig,
A blister in the leaf!

To celebrate what's been
Those whom the god dislikes
Accept the golden noun
And know it brilliant there
As a bare javelin.

They truly stand aside:
Like the encircling dead
Look, hear the judgement, but
Love what alive they loved,
Apart, at one with it.

FOR A HOUSE OF FRIENDS

May the sun so build over whatever hill
    You lean a shoulder on
As I saw him this morning, due at your door and sill,
    Array benediction

There by a winterburned bush and the March fields,
    Again lassoing
A particular ground and shelter of what is
    Loved and pursuing.

Light, of all voices with which we are spoken to
    No sweeter tone,
Addressing your eavesdropping roof, and the half of day
    Ready by the east down;

Not useless to invoke blessing already come
    But to its well
And presence here to accord recognition,
    Words: let them tell.

PASTORAL

We did not climb low Bredon but by Elmley Castle lay.
When summer and an afternoon foresaw no likely end
We watched, from a shadow, haymakers making hay,
The rear wheel of a fallen cycle slowly cease to spin.
In the village, where we mounted to the top of the church tower
We could scan the Malvern line: the alabaster dead
Snug by their effigies and quartered arms below.
Someone had scored the outline of his shoe against the lead
Roof [squaretoed and Puritan] upon just such a day,
Worried with king and Cromwell as we with Germany,
And bored at being young.
Then in the long declining of the light into the cool
Exhaustion of a midland evening we rode for good away
By the umbelliferae-feathered lanes we came;
A part of the equation of nothing happening on a day
When this field was mowed, that harvest corn stood higher,
Of similar summer events we are led to rejoice in, while
The loving, responsible and occluded power
Achieves his anomalous purposes with a smile.

THE LONG BARROWS

Tump, barrow, tumulus; all their names are
    Evocative of those tombs
Set on the high bare places, looking over
    Our valleys tamed and changed

Whose woods have fallen into square and hedgerow
    Or branch-line villages;
Whose hill-bent horizon, less sweet than now,
    Dragged, harshlier serrated.

Bones long dissolved, and iron ornament,
    Whatever weapon, shield,
Oxidised to a scar, the monument
    Of sadder ground's availed.

Should I look westward here to Bredon, Malvern,
    Comforted by those names,
On the right hand the Meon hill strides empty
    Behind the blackening land

At which these knolled and too long dead list greenly
    From aboriginal
Unalien or alien ground; and baldly
    Divert the triumphal.

NOVEMBER 1956

Stirrup to stirrup, not authority, but
    Attached to power
(And like, as the world over, expensive bars
    Are like each other,

Some vicious, some not, but the same boredom
    And more or less expense),
I see the stupid bearing down the stupid
    By a glum residence

Of government: police mounted in the pride
    Of delegated
Licence to violence, and disciplined,
    Break the egotistic.

Sparkling down Whitehall I perceive the riding
    Guardians of obedience;
– A loose illusory crowd dispersing
    Moral coincidence –

Each 'I want' scrubbed out by a bigger 'We
    Have now decided'.
Whatever the question or the capital,
    Here as I see it

Is impotence of the individual
    For love or hate;
And, above that impotence, the voluble
    Combine of state

Unable with horses, batons, guns, machines.
    For a cry 'I' I cry.
Valid in bleak formation stroll the hosts,
    Absolute today;

Valid in bleak formation: and, viable,
    Harmless among smoke,
A broken person clutching at a broken
    Promise to speak or break.

UPON A MARRIAGE ANNIVERSARY

Now, on the anniversary of not our love
But of our believing, I may speak for you
(Who, alive and loving, in the next room breathe,
Passion communing in the act with faith)

Sentence of affirmation, sentence of praise
To honour best the particular creature
In the love and mercy of what is:
Unarguable as grief or happiness

To the opposing evil to oppose
The impossible – faith that cannot prove
But asserts the government of a Love,

As by a marriage vow we did,
Till upon a horizon in the East
A cloud assumes the image of a rose.

A LEAVE-TAKING

GORDON ALFRED WRIGHT, 1891–1957

Coming away from a farewell, from the last Good-bye,
I turn from an air terminus into a sparkle of rain
Unable now, and it is for ever, to look back or say.

Among multitudes on Waterloo Bridge and each alone
Reflect such partings are worse than dying: too violently
The imperfect communication of blood and bone

Becomes no longer even probable: what joy
Such as the living feel at surviving decease
Is there to lighten with a lefthanded gaiety,

Or at all to relieve these occasions of distress?
Shouldering through unmemorable crowds of no love
On a way home to now strange familiarities,

Reflect in addition that the word is Forgive
We have to say to whom we love, and who own ours.
The damage done one to another by those who live

Fingering the heart always in the parting hours.
September 3, 1956

AT THE DEATH OF ROY CAMPBELL

Since of your kind so few
This world affords, not now may we afford
Equably to lose or let by
You, the quarry and quarrel of so many
Qualities, with the hour in discord.

Do the vainglorious
Trail a glory after their vanity?
For, so you may have shown to us,
Horseman and soldier, the vicarious
Nature of pride in a well of humility.

How does the poem move?
Concerned with justice it presents judgement.
Impelled by love it says 'I love'.
Thus, and by these presents, can never prove
Anything but its own allegiance.

How may its poet live
Under its public its private dominion
Addressed to energies
That, never fully nor truly disclosed to us,
Assert in language transcending assertion?

There are no answers,
No final answers – yours as good as any:
Swagger cloak and black Cordoba
Worn over a mention in despatches
By the general Quiepo de Llana.

A mask. The mask becomes
As all who wear it warn, the man that wears it.
Yet, moulded behind it, beyond
Attribution, invisible, the expression
Language is given to elicit.

Lie where it was let drop,
Violence grinning on Portuguese ground!
Let me speak what below it beat –
First I name gentleness of the stopped heart
And its humility second.

Naming, I elegise
You, Sir, with coldness, whom I do love and loved;
And, being Africa's,
Say the first lover of her European muse
Is by her Iberian peninsula buried.

I

A NOTE TO THE CHOREOGRAPHER
WALTER GORE

Dear Sir, you employ language
The great abstractions understand;
Torso, arm, and thigh engage
Gesture with an eye and hand
Till, silent, the huge poems rise
Between the black wings of a stage
Where, Sir, your images devise
What dances in our dying cage.
And may assuage.

II

POSTCARD FROM VENICE

TO STEPHEN SPENDER

Those golden riderless horses yaw
As over the green floor of a bay
Easy at hawsers, while the air
Rides that unbeaten piazza;
Venice descending to our day
Suspends European glory here.

Lagooned, eternal as an hour,
We saw that lily where she lay
Afloat unfolding to the sea
Her fading summaries of power
At nightfall, and, hovering there
Like dusk, the unhinged energies.

Archangels beating up a wave
San Marco crumbles into stone,
Pierce desolation brooding on
The lovely city, dove by dove,
With declarations of the power
That drew a Venus from the foam

III

CORNWALL

Nothing more ruined there
Than a balancing rock
The memnon to nowhere:
A horn of nothing, bent to crack,
Yawns, and itself refills –
Fields cropped by the nightmare!
O waters undermined!
O long stones heavier
Than a horizon or than men!
The seal-ridden water
Knocks at such places
But they outgrind the sea
Like grief, or like peasants.

IV

LINES FOR A GODCHILD

TO ISEULT MARY CRONIN

Iseult, I make for you
No unlucky wishes
For heart or feature,
But leave their future to
Your father, your mother,
And your own nature.
Love individual
Than cup or poem
So much the longer shall
Stand in your room
And, shining harder than
Silver or syllable,
Really belong to you.
As the globe edges by
Its usual disasters
You, with birth completed,
Face the consequences:
The growing, and ageing,
And loving, and raging,
And boredom, and dying.
Respect all these: wage
That life with courage.

V

ON ANOTHER GRECIAN URN

FOR DRUMMOND ALLISON AND OTHERS

Transfixed adolescence on a vase!
By a too early dying, you
Whom I commemorate and kissed
Here utter nothing can be worse
Not even humiliation of
Being alive, than being dead.
What stone is reared, what stone, what cross
But blood worrying at a heart?
If I don't remember, who will,
That little dirt and broken skull –
The public of the dryasdust?

VI

OF THE POET

I am a man like you but I look and hark
For if I don't I will not hear the god speak.
And what does the god talk about? God knows.
He names what exists, or, appearing in space
Like an atom of hydrogen from nowhere,
Manifests a principle of energy.

VII

TO THE OTHERS

God commanded men to love
Else there would be, God knows,
Even less love than there is
Now between us, otherwise.
I, obeying God, must love;
You, dear sirs, do as you please,
As you like be damned or not.

AN INVOCATION TO THE GODDESS

O sea born and obscene
Venus I see ascend
Fishbright upon a shell
Out of a salty pool
Angels and flesh attend,
The dolphin-sewn and blown
Mirrors of sea surround
As bawdy as a boy
That blank desirous form.
The goddess smiles from joy,
I look her in the groin;
Her seakale coloured eyes
Acknowledge her concern.
Not the ideal but real
Half sheltered by her hand,
Sty of ambiguities
Offensive and divine.
Venus preferring joy
Defenceless from the sea
Attending to defend,
Feminine, debonair,
Step naked to the shore.
Step, wound in your hair,
And singing galleries
Fish, fowl, flesh, surround you.
I cry your worshipper
Upon this island ground
Down by a sky and still
Crying borne by a sea,
Rejected and acclaimed.
Announce perfection, smile
Upon what is deformed,
Accept what is, and be.
Beach, beach your scallop here
By pillars of a sea
Whose black-backed dolphins plunge,
Plunge and thrash salty hair.

MONOLOGUE OF A DEAF MAN

Et lui comprit trop bien, n'ayant pas entendu.
TRISTAN CORBIÈRE

It is a good plan, and began with childhood
As my fortune discovered, only to hear
How much it is necessary to have said.
Oh silence, independent of a stopped ear,
You observe birds, flying, sing with wings instead.

Then do you console yourself? You are consoled
If you are, as all are. So easy a youth
Still unconcerned with the concern of a world
Where, masked and legible, a moment of truth
Manifests what, gagged, a tongue should have told;

Still observer of vanity and courage
And of these mirror as well; that is something
More than a sound of violin to assuage
What the human being most dies of: boredom
Which makes hedgebirds clamour in their blackthorn cage.

But did the brushless fox die of eloquence?
No, but talked himself, it seems, into a tale.
The injury, dominated, is an asset;
It is there for domination, that is all.
Else what must faith do deserted by mountains?

Talk to me then, you who have so much to say,
Spectator of the human conversation,
Reader of tongues, examiner of the eye,
And detective of clues in every action,
What could a voice, if you heard it, signify?

The tone speaks less than a twitch and a grimace.
People make to depart, do not say 'Goodbye'.
Decision, indecision, drawn on every face
As if they spoke. But what do they really say?
You are not spared, either, the banalities.

In whatever condition, whole, blind, dumb,
One-legged or leprous, the human being is,
I affirm the human condition is the same,
The heart half broken in ashes and in lies,
But sustained by the immensity of the divine.

Thus I too must praise out of a quiet ear
The great creation to which I owe I am
My grief and my love. O hear me if I cry
Among the din of birds deaf to their acclaim
Involved like them in the not unhearing air.

VERSES TO ST CECILIA

Inventress and virgin,
Martyred Cecilia,
Cecilia intervene:
Sustaining audience
Hear, as I cannot hear
In disordered silence.

Cecilia there is none:
No silence any where
As zithering each zephyr
Leaves of a hawthorn tells,
Or dog out of water
Shaking a head of bells.
Though slow galaxies crawl
And hold a note so long
Eternity alone
Is audient to their chime,
Yet still on a black stream
Pulses their wailing swarm.
Sound being action, I,
Golden Cecilia,
Have seen the instruments
Of music move in praise
Subduing the silence
With a stroke of violins,
And opposing cymbals
Their holy temples raise.
Still, still your organpipes
Dumb under nave or aisle
There without motion draw
Blind music from the air
With not a single tone
To blunder on my ear
Of a congregation.
Among your stalactites
Cecilia I affirm
There is no silence, none.
The quiet is a glass

Reflecting eyes of stone.
What noise would be here?
Whence should that music come?
What spirit moves the air
Or entropy unseen
Commands my 'I believe'?
O certain paradox
O double paradigm
Entreating the divine!
Blessed Cecilia
Wholly the deaf must praise
Wholly the dumb shall tell.
The unseen government
Shall be made visible
And unknown music raise.

A THANKSGIVING

The living, the living, shall praise thee.

I

The octosyllabic verse and I
Have never hit it off together;
I wobble like a seaside bather
Astraddle on a very airy
Pegasus of rubber, when
The impredictable seas are high.

Therefore I, in order to obey,
Invent a poem and its laws
Coasting the eight and vocable shoals
To discover what I never see;
And, mounting an artificial horse
Of my self assembled, bob away.

Yet let him sprout wings from each shoulder
When it is necessary to fly.
To her this miracle I may leave
Whom I must love because I love her:
Have the seasonable muse and I
Not, on occasion, kissed each other?

So without further preamble I'll
Plunge in the middle of my matter
And, lighting on its broken water,
Begin the poem in such a style
As this: The year was 1950
When I, prepared for an arrival,

Arrived at a transfiguring.
I mean that possession which returns
But easily may never come
(So many energies conspiring)
When once the spiritual irons
Dislink and fall, to tumble clattering.

Delayed adolescence, I derive
No satisfaction looking at you
Any more than Pygmalion who
Contemplates, before it comes alive,
The marble that, not yet a statue,
Groans for the limbs his chisel gives.

There, secure within a crystal vein,
Implicit, inarticulate, sleeps
The internal, hidden, fatal face
Anticipating an eternal reign
Of marble, mortal in an eclipse –
Keeps time and silence in the stone.

Cold midland centre of my boyhood,
Where, level with the Nen, each flashing
Summer would pile the agony on:
Deaf, inadequate, far from good,
I wandered with some others, aching,
Stunted in a stunted neighbourhood;

Creased sullen thoroughfares, and people
Outside a Saturday cinema
Too familiar with grief to meet her,
Bored as a wheelchair with its cripple,
Excruciate like an enema
Or stab the cheek as a green apple –

The usual memories of youth.
As free as a caterpillar in
Its homespun chrysalis I gambolled,
– Ambitious to break away and loath –
Till, half aware what I was doing,
So larks might fall, I opened my mouth.

Lasting, hieroglyphic, and aloud,
Inherited and subject to change,
Obeying your self created laws;
As vague as a mountain in its shroud
Where the half clouded frontiers hinge;
With the voices of no where endowed

That pierce a midnight like a nerve
Crying of nothing and of all things;
All language I worship – in special
That which I utter and may observe,
Who gives to me apparel and sings,
Whose path I may help prepare, I serve.

Else such intelligence as we have
Would, blinded, atrophy and perish
Without a word, like a naked babe:
Given the genetic gift of gab,
All other attributes will nourish
And even flourish beyond a grave.

The oval vocables rolling in
Silence surrounding an eye and ear
Beauty superseded and increased
With a round din of praise extolling
What had been created or achieved,
What imagined or what befallen.

Thus little as the tannery smell;
Or the handpocketed corner boys;
The bleary uniform of windows;
Dead, belly-up roach in the canal;
Or the common rag-hatched children's sores;
Did I regard the natural vernal

Magnificence of the country side
When, the river carrying like a shield
His intense glittering arms of gold
In the alluvial valley, rode
The late spring by some yet undefiled
Ways heavy with half a summer's shade.

As a fish in an aquarium
Inhabits a gallery, but moves
In an environment of water,
Apparently with the lookers-on
Consorting, yet separately lives
In a transparent division,

So in as deaf a world I wandered
Throughout the cruellest period:
That time of life when we are given
Weapons of manhood but are hindered
By even the fear of seeming odd
(No less than by ignorance sundered)

From their employment. How can we know,
Barking our shins against our passion,
That there is really no occasion
For the tears of vanity to flow?
As for me, unable to believe
In the banal that, like oil, allows

People and engines to continue
Unseized, you may imagine how I
Wetted my solitary pillow
Each midnight, and with what a dew.
Yet the grapes, I guessed, were not so sour,
As, tasting, later, I found true.

Apolitical and innocent,
Convoyed through unguided public years
Our fathers' comminatory blood
Made possible on a western front,
As unliable as unallied
And knowing that we were ignorant;

Most ignorant however of
The communication of the human
And of the idiom of an ear,
We by abnormal dialogues proved
They were, in language and in passion,
A handshake given without a glove;

How not a voice but a face behaves
Became an object of the eye
We turned to the living world that wags
And by a quivering hair betrays
Where noise and intelligence lie,
Where a wind, or life, or danger is.

Deaf companions I do not pity,
To whom I dedicate no lies,
Over those gulfs of understanding
Divide, divided by society,
The real infirmity that divides;
Who suffer and who are not sorry,

Between whom and me the word is really
At last, at last, a barricade –
Forgive the gilt with which I cover
Our disaster that is not wholly
Ours or disaster, but is made
In your humility and courage holy.

II

To this objective correlative
I own a personal attachment,
Thus cannot speak with mere detachment
Of even so largely dead a self;
By sad college barges I see him
Engarlanded with autumnal leaf

While a slow, blind October Isis
Laps slackly from under Folly Bridge
On the way to a salter water.
Memory, fish or siren, rises
Scallop-bottomed from a winter sedge,
Carries a mirror of devices.

Here, stifled, hung from every tower
The clustered and illustrious bells:
Aphonic Magdalen, Oriel, Tom,
Merton, Carfax, St Mary's spire,
Barren of sussuration
Because a war as well as I came there.

Or floodlit by a visiting moon
Between the rivers seemed to hover,

To veer and flower like wheeling doves,
A baroque statement uttered from
Some breeding moveless domes and towers,
Cajoling knowledge: of wisdom

Affirming. Then a perfect summer
Wept willow over gliddering punts,
The hills suspended in their purple;
The brandished chestnuts dripped their honour
Slowly, while further than a fable
Dull drummed a buzz of distant armour.

Late, late, the lovers on the ground
Lay dallying as delaying stars
Burnt over hedges thick and sappy,
Till, long-lost, they to bodies turned;
Noon-dazed, the season shed its hours
For ever with far destruction armed;

Lush as melodrama, halcyon
That summer! And where are you now,
Buried in sand or avoirdupois,
You swimmers, beautiful and dying,
Of the same summer? Especially you
Struck by a muse, by her forsaken?

Hung up in the shapeless event of
The stupidity of too many,
You, so conscripted, flew off to die
Without the flatfooted, blind, or deaf.
Spectator, uncommitted, I
Saw mysterious exaction prove

Exactly nothing except the sum
You actually were prepared to pay:
In that final surrender of choice
Enough of good blood and boredom
For an applepie bed in the sky,
Your satisfactory return.

Thus, choicelessly irresponsible,
And from what affected me apart,
Through no inherent virtue I
Stood by to watch the actual
As usual in abstraction die;
But educed a facet of the real

Winking from the firework display.
The mysterious which girds itself
There (but nowhere more effectively
Than in an ordinary day)
Yet, unveiling, hid protectively
Its shade within a shadow, lay

Ambushed. Like a stage cat I altered
With a mere irrelevance the scene
By walking on undominated
While Timon or a Hamlet faltered;
The assurance of a tragic queen
In the oblivious self-centred

Acknowledgement of my own concerns.
Though I no more than a cat might know
What those concerns concerned: a riddle
I investigate in cynic terms,
As one believing that to fiddle
Is to be not idle when Rome burns.

So let me celebrate here the dead
As who most preserve our memories
Like flies in amber; of flying youth,
Of all that then we were, did, and said,
Accusers ignorant of new lies:
The equal guardians, and never laid.

'An impostor, but with so much love
That I forgive him' I hear describe
Sidney who bore the keys among us,
Whose proper desert picked his grave:
In whose face I learned to recognize
Justice elevating the visage

He had elected (and yet not he,
The talent in his fingers lying).
Cold, famous, recondite, and clever,
More short of time than most of money,
Well for so many till the dying
He wore a gesture of to die.

A fallen interval of snow
Edged in his memory as in mine
With sharpness, a lien of the spring,
Led me acknowledge and so avow
And, avowing, henceforth to define,
His vocation that was mine also.

The trees which bore that weight of winter
Erect in ordinary groves
The arms and heads we have forgotten,
The silver branches we stood under
Unaltered by decades of leaves
Since from below their shining lintel

– O no recognition then! but now
How easily I see diverging
The tracks that led, the ways dividing! –
We turned to watch upon those fallow
Fields our parallel and emerging
Fresh footmarks print the fallen snow.

Spent as a rower at an oar
Slid by each sullener afternoon:
Chapped, ermine, square, divided fields
Fixed in their hibernal languor,
– Hag-ridden when a glittering moon
Shot overhead her unshielding car

And Orion, brooched, assumed the sky
Above all sentinels to look down
Upon a European colophon
Sparkling in bright artillery.
Then that searchlit amphitheatre
Of systems, fading into day,

As if to declare ephemeral
Just causes and combat, or to shroud
By diffusing slowly into cloud
The juster irony from us all,
The cursive of a fighting sky
Held Aeolian and aerial.

III

An old man upon his deathbed said
To those about him, 'When I recall
My youth irrecoverably spent
It is not purgatory that I dread,
But I gnaw my elbow in torment
At the boundless mercy of my God:

For that infinite forgiveness flays
Not any thing that I ever did,
In rendering sin thus invalid
Through his compassion and his grace:
But from temptation resisted and
Sin I omitted, he turns his face.'

Not what I undid but left undone
I have to mourn when I look behind:
Not mourn my positive idleness
My lizard dallying in the sun,
But all those occasions which demand
The actual prudence of action

When, marginal and a Londoner,
In the summer trebled evenings
Among the maimed and the uniformed
From Soho bar to Soho bar
I milled, while iron convenings
Got on with a poltergeist war –

Timid as a shellfish and unbored
To observe the talking drinkers down

Their halves. Unconversant and alone
I noted all that I never heard,
Divining, for I saw it happen,
What beyond a silence had occurred;

Since by hearing nothing I became
A glass to every one who turned
Towards me, and like a mirror threw
Their inverse images back at them.
They smiled; and I, a mercury, drew
Upon glass a smile above the bone;

Then pity, vanity, or courage
In each face spoke. But each mouth expelled,
Dumb, moving, words unarmed to move
The one who, constrained to envisage
Alternate clues, compelled to prove
In personal silence, language.

O long and derelict streets I still
Appear to wander in, you remain.
Memory leaves you marbled over
And, violable as viable
To each far gone and valid lover,
Stares where I nightly kept vigil: –

Stand at the bar and that ghost betray
Twisting about his glass of bitter
Images with no word to utter
Whom cowardice made a stander-by.
His own fear was killer of his own.
He will understand what you say.

  'For his first love he fetched a reason
  And there he set it where she was laid
  To be a key to that misprision
  But she took his metal up and said
  O I want a comb my locks to braid
  They will never answer to a key
  Go further off by my side to be,

(55)

'To another he came in season
By a large indifference conveyed
To her luxurious liaison
That nothing he did not want denied
But limped from the unflowering bed
Of satisfaction to hear her say
Go further off by my side to be.

'Then to a last he offered treason
Wide open upon a plate instead
And so he laid the ghostly vision
She took his hand and he shook his head
And there alloying the unallayed
She crossed his palm with the given key
Go further off by my side to be.'

So, flagging flagstaff of a pinnace,
Let now your sky-ploughing timber ride –
Rock, rock with bellying canvas brailed,
Loving to make a plus of minus –
By every creek and haven sailed
In service of beckoning Venus.

Then, a scapegoat in sheep's clothing, I
Confounded but conveyed no alarm
To huddled abattoir-loving sheep
In valleys and pauses where they lay,
Nor knew a wilderness for my home,
My safety in no security:

Nor did that vision easily break
Over the soft mahogany bars
Where, hoping to be a someone else,
I taught a solitude how to speak.
Realization is a royal coach
Action and suffering must precede.

The sacrifice that the god will have
On some one other heaviest weighs:
Not on oneself but always those
We most love, whose hurt we least forget;

For the jealous and divine refuse
Any but an undivided love

Till, bound by bitterness and self-hate,
Those new purposes we perform
That parallel and transcend our own,
That we do not initiate.
Thus what possesses and inspires
Is not an ecstasy but a guilt.

Yet the argument of the poem sings
Against what desires to condemn,
And, blinder than music in the air,
States and repeats the IS that wrings
Echo and answer from despair;
Or, with collapsed and rutilant wings

Alighting upon an intellect
Preens in her guttering plumage there.
Who understands what he must obey?
The causes quarrel with effect.
I seize the peregrine falcon where
Her settling wingbeat shall elect.

First chosen, then dedicated, then
So committed that, for bad or good,
The contract, liable to occlude
Each former will and disposition,
Resembles that of matrimony –
Perhaps allowing separation

But not envisaging a divorce.
Each in the toils of language
Betrays, embraces, or defeats
A muse's naked grievances;
Or, with intolerable anguish
(A black Douglas with the heart of Bruce)

Javelins among his enemies
Far from his purpose or from his home
His light, insupportable burden,

Which he follows and in seeking dies.
Thus his purposes are not his own
But, like unmourning atlantes,

Bear (their corroded eyeballs down
Bent to the base) a total weight
Poised by a designing architect
Whose monument is to them unknown,
And what flowering cupolas erect
Or may not over the standing stone.

To the unapparent I submit
As any sailor any day
Confides to an ambiguous sea
He cannot count upon, his ship.
I see my ignorance and my skill
Cockle on the shallow and the deep

Vicissitude of that breathing shell.
I believe my instruments, believe
A pilot chart or the seamark raised
Which may confirm navigable
That sound the plundering garboard seized:
But bind my trust to the miracle

Binnacled over dead and lonely
Unfathering wildernesses where
The signs that no one can read are set
In a clouded sky and a salt sea,
For those who do not know where they are
Nor where they came from or would be.

IV

On a glass floated the painted quay,
And above our foremast a seagull
As if he recognized that harbour
Broke one wing and bent back to sea.
Focused, the glistening houses pull
Their borough uphill from the bay:

Behind our shoulders the morning light
Scattered its angels on home and hill
By the blue pillars of breakfast smoke,
Ghosts of bamboo rising to one height.
As a town clock struck at eight o'clock,
The bollard bit our hawser bight.

We landed after a short voyage.
In a still, hammering air, the sun
Hoisted to a zenith hour by hour
Over Eire green as a mirage.
There we wandered in a snakeless June
About her blarneying foliage,

Burned gaols and brokendown palaces,
Menhirs of the memorable kings:
A smile of habitual despair
Affecting as an eternal peace
Leaned from her rotten towers, or
A witherless artificial wreath.

A dome as unspeckled as a swan
Dreamed on her damp and flickering woods:
The greenroom island gleamed below a
Soft but a thunder-dowering sun.
Then, happy to be going nowhere,
We lay on a crackling bed of fern

Garbed in some stars and laid grief away.
Responsibility at our side,
We saw the necessary become
No less difficult or easy
But finally that which must be done:
A question echoing a reply.

Where, between us and our actual home,
Spun the cold web of a nightlong sea
That held the floating keels and spread
With green arms the miles and the hours from
Our assembly with the poleaxed dead,
Below a transfixed bower, and blown

By the secret airs, all night we lay
At loss while unsleeping birds sang on
In wavering keys, rejoiced to sing
In darkness against an expected day,
As for the known coming of a king
So to precur him on his way.

Now I cast memory to that place
I can go back to – as all maps show
The same winds walk and the same trees grow –
I understand better where I was.
The leaves lie dead and the short groves wait
For the possession of a voice.

May it inhabit me when I look
From this real table towards a world
Where wickedness rides the saddle-galled
Foolsback of the human to the dark,
With love, forsaking and forsaken,
That never in the end forsook;

Cry over the acclaim of silence
In the long box when at last I hear
What I so far have listened for.
My single virtue a compliance
To the wind when I felt it blow
And the mastery of a bias

I shall never wholly know.
I see the leaves utter with their tongues
Their untransliteratable speech,
Hear that ocean waters quarrel to,
Which, pounding upon a sweaty beach
Affirms its glory of being so;

I see the human being divide
Between 'I destroy' and 'I make'
The bone his liberty weeps upon;
The worshipping brute, divine and sad,
Because he knows what he has done
But not the breast where he may hide.

Here number, illuminate, approve,
Patroness of the human tongue,
These concepts we must move among –
Blind shadows flickering in a cave.
I believe in this resurrection:
That if I speak, then I shall live.

And by that nature which I do not
Either understand or perceive
Entirely, because all words possess
More than the meaning that we allot,
I find all speech becoming praise.
All things I name when I look about,

Offences, imbecilities, are
No less than antelopes and lilies
Or the actions of the beautiful,
Caught up in the catalogue of prayer.
For how can I condemn evil
Without a thanksgiving it is there?

VALEDICTION

Absurd and dying muse
Haltered who may return
In what guise I don't know
By more difficult ways
Now an overtoppled sun
Whirs burning to its home:
That I may recognize
Under a hod or pillar
Asseverant, eternal,
That visage of image;
Have verses to align
A few stones to your house;
I am to beg. Exact
Manifest and betray
What is at most begotten
Among small passion, small
Discomfort and desire;
Betray the exaltation.
Which of us walks toward
The other when we meet
Is of no matter nor
The perhaps burdened pace;
Obey the recognition.
Give me the word to make
I have to give you best.